~A BINGO BOOK~

Story Elements Bingo Book

COMPLETE BINGO GAME IN A BOOK

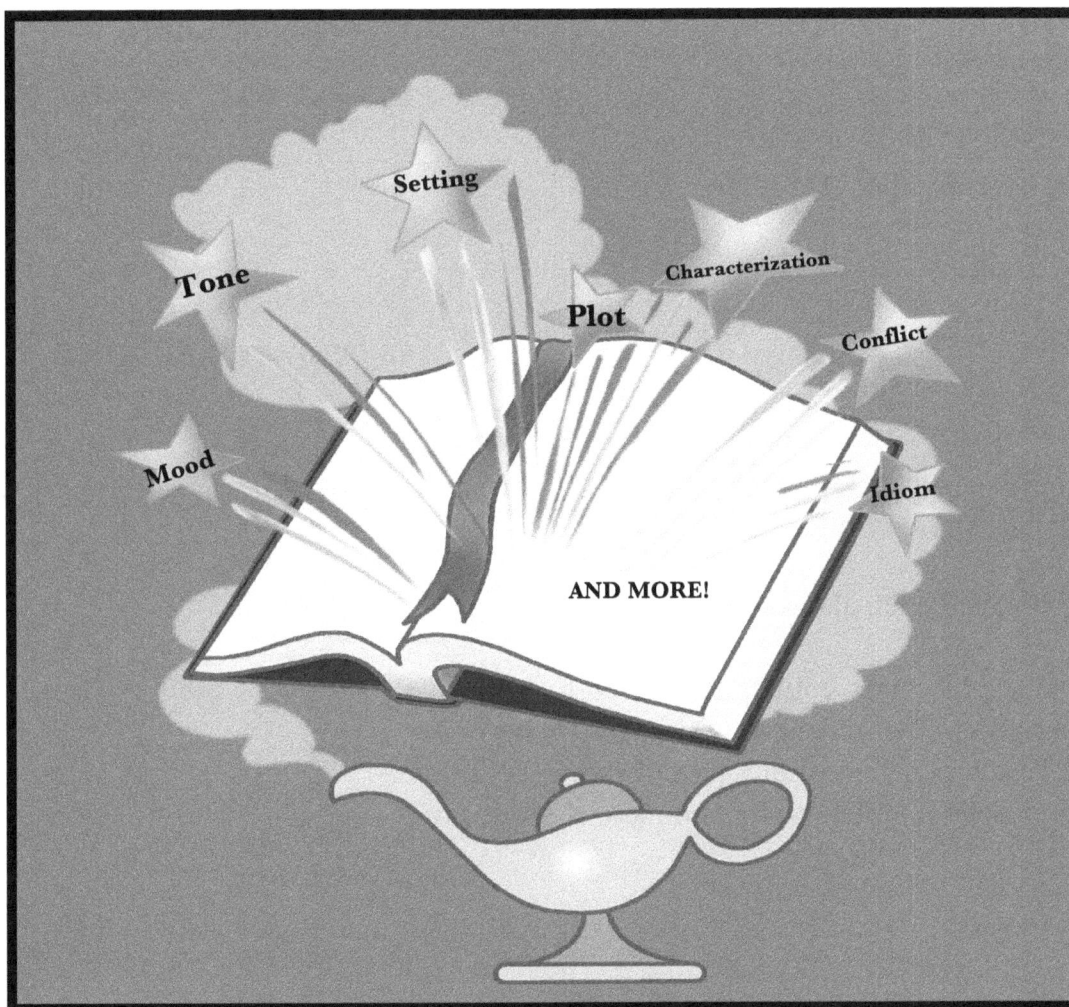

Setting

Tone

Characterization

Plot

Conflict

Mood

Idiom

AND MORE!

Written By Rebecca Stark

Educational Books 'n' Bingo

ISBN 978-0-87386-547-0

Educational Books 'n' Bingo

Printed in the U.S.A.

ELEMENTS OF LITERATURE BINGO
Directions

INCLUDED:

List of Terms

Templates for Additional Terms and Clues

2 Clues per Term

30 Unique Bingo Cards

Markers

1. **Either cut apart the book or make copies of ALL the sheets. You might want to make an extra copy of the clue sheets to use for introduction and review. Keep the sheets in an envelope for easy reuse.**

2. Cut apart the call cards with terms and clues.

3. Pass out one bingo card per student. There are enough for a class of 30.

4. Pass out markers. You may cut apart the markers included in this book or use any other small items of your choice.

5. Decide whether or not you will require the entire card to be filled. Requiring the entire card to be filled provides a better review. However, if you have a short time to fill, you may prefer to have them do the just the border or some other format. Tell the class before you begin what is required.

6. There are 50 topics. Read the list before you begin. If there are any topics that have not been covered in class, you may want to read to the students the topic and clues before you begin.

7. There is a blank space in the middle of each card. You can instruct the students to use it as a free space or you can write in answers to cover topics not included. Of course, in this case you would create your own clues. (Templates provided.)

8. Shuffle the cards and place them in a pile. Two or three clues are provided for each topic. If you plan to play the game with the same group more than once, you might want to choose a different clue for each game. If not, you may choose to use more than one clue.

9. Be sure to keep the cards you have used for the present game in a separate pile. When a student calls, "Bingo," he or she will have to verify that the correct answers are on his or her card AND that the markers were placed in response to the proper questions. Pull out the cards that are on the student's card keeping them in the order they were used in the game. Read each clue as it was given and ask the student to identify the correct answer from his or her card.

10. If the student has the correct answers on the card AND has shown that they were marked in response to the *correct questions,* then that student is the winner and the game is over. If the student does not have the correct answers on the card OR he or she marked the answers in response to *the wrong questions,* then the game continues until there is a proper winner.m, and there are enough unique "cards" for 30 students!

11. If you want to play again, reshuffle the cards and begin again.

Have fun!

TERMS

ALLUSION	IMAGERY
ANTAGONIST	INFERENCE
AUTHOR	IRONY
BIOGRAPHY	LITERATURE
CHARACTER	METAPHOR
CHARACTERIZATION	MOOD
CLASSICS	NARRATOR
CLIFFHANGER	NOVEL
CLIMAX	PLOT
CONFLICT	POINT OF VIEW
CONNOTATION	PROLOGUE
DÉNOUEMENT	PROSE
DIALECT	PROTAGONIST
DIALOGUE	SATIRE
DRAMA	SCIENCE FICTION
EPIC	SEQUENCE
EPILOGUE	SETTING
EXPOSITION	STEREOTYPE
FANTASY	STYLE
FIGURATIVE LANGUAGE	SUBPLOT
FLASHBACK	SUSPENSE
FOIL	SYMBOL
FORESHADOWING	THEME
GENRES (Literary)	TONE
HISTORICAL FICTION	TRAITS

Additional Terms

Choose as many additional terms as you would like and write them in the squares.
Repeat each as desired.
Cut out the squares and randomly distribute them to the class.
Instruct the students to place their square on the center space of their card.

Clues for Additional Terms

Write three clues for each of your additional terms.

_____ 1. 2. 3.	_____ 1. 2. 3.
_____ 1. 2. 3.	_____ 1. 2. 3.
_____ 1. 2. 3.	_____ 1. 2. 3.

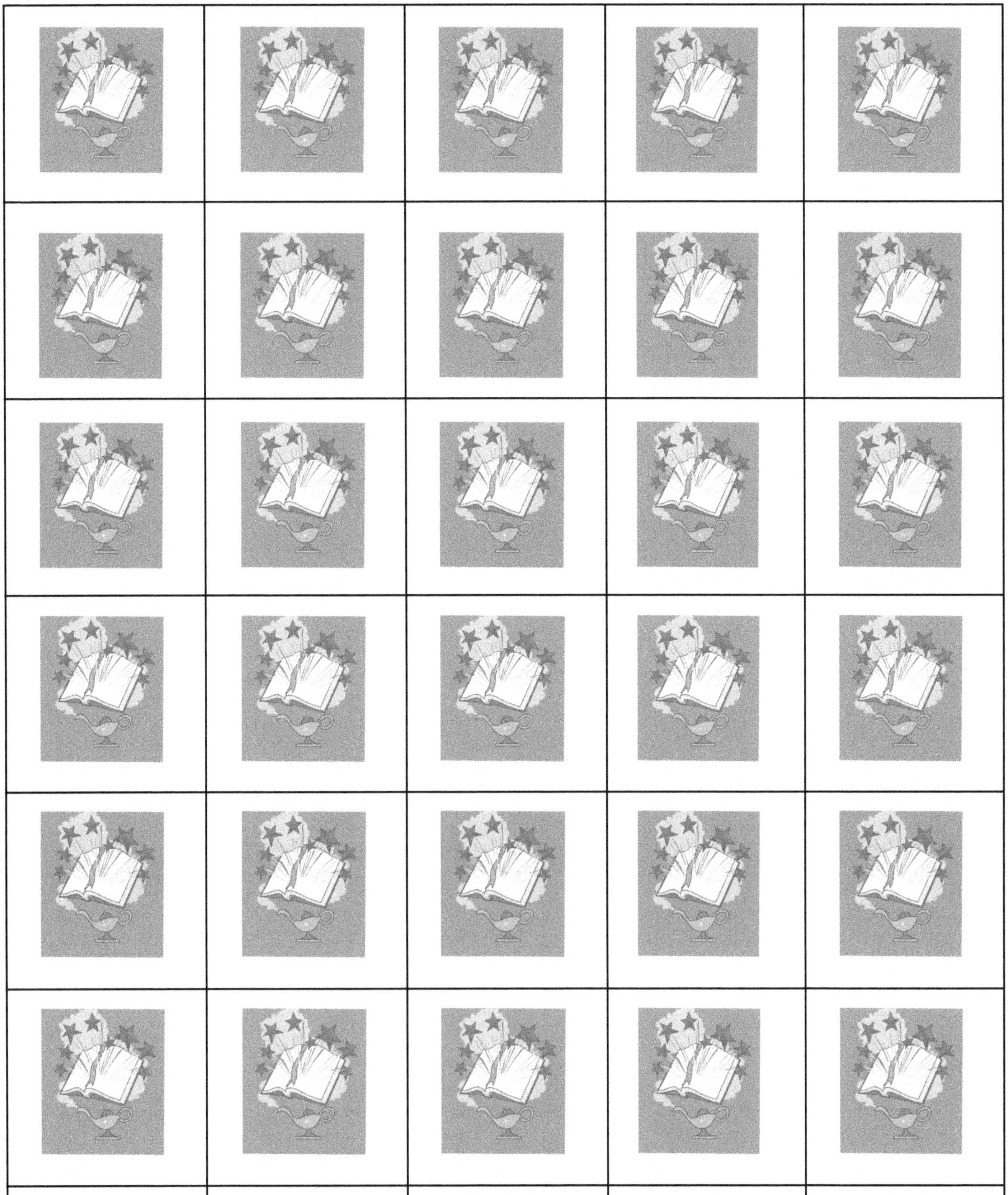

Allusion
1. This is a reference in a literary work to something outside of the work.
2. If you referred to someone as a Scrooge, you would be using this literary device.
3. In *Romeo and Juliet,* Montague's reference to Aurora, the Roman goddess of the dawn, is an example of this.

Antagonist
1. The adversary of the main character might be called this.
2. Its antonym is *protagonist.*
3. If the hero of the story is the protagonist, then the villain is this.

Author
1. The writer of a literary work is called this.
2. Charles Dickens is the ___ of *A Christmas Carol, Oliver Twist* and other novels.
3. Many people believe that William Shakespeare was the greatest English ___.

Biography
1. This is a type of nonfiction literature.
2. *Amos Fortune, Free Man,* by Elizabeth Yates, is one that was awarded a Newbery Medal.
3. If you write one about yourself, add the prefix "auto-."

Character
1. A static one stays pretty much the same throughout the work.
2. A dynamic one changes in an important way during the work.
3. A flat one is not fully developed; a round one is.

Characterization
1. It is the method used by an author to develop a character.
2. It is how the author conveys to the readers a character's personality, values, physical attributes, and other traits.
3. It refers to the literary techniques that writers use to develop a character.

Classics
1. This term refers to works of enduring excellence.
2. *The Adventures of Tom Sawyer, A Tale of Two Cities, Don Quixote,* and *Moby Dick* are among the works considered this.
3. This term can also refer to the study of the literary works of ancient Greece and Rome in particular.

Cliffhanger
1. It sometimes refers to a suspenseful situation at the end of a chapter.
2. Authors use this device at the end of chapters to make us wonder what will happen next.
3. The term may refer to a serial or melodrama in which each episode ends in suspense.

Climax
1. It is the point of greatest emotional tension. At this point the reader may know who will win the conflict.
2. It is the major turning point in a story.
3. It is the point in the plot at which the action reverses from rising to falling.

Conflict
1. It is the struggle that occurs between opposing forces in a plot.
2. This struggle may be between characters, between a character and society or between a character and nature.
3. This struggle within the plot may also be a character's struggle with himself.

Connotation
1. It is the associated meaning of a word or a phrase.
2. An antonym is *denotation,* or the clearly expressed meaning of a word or phrase.
3. The word *slender* has a positive one for most people; the word *skinny* has a negative one for most.

Dénouement
1. It is another word for the resolution of the plot.
2. It is a French term meaning "unraveling" or "unknotting."
3. It follows the climax of the plot.

Dialect
1. It is language that is characteristic of a particular region or group.
2. This excerpt from *Treasure Island,* by Stevenson, is an example of it: "This is a handy cove, and a pleasant sittyated grog-shop."
3. This excerpt from *The Adventures of Tom Sawyer,* by Twain, is an example of it: "Tom, it was middling warm in school, warn't it?"

Dialogue
1. It is the spoken words between characters in a literary work.
2. It is the conversation between characters in a drama or narrative.
3. This gives a literary work a more conversational flow.

Drama
1. This word is derived from the Greek word *dran,* meaning "to do" or "to perform."
2. This literary work is designed for performance by actors in a theater.
3. This type of work is sometimes called a play.

Epic
1. It is a long narrative poem.
2. *The Iliad* and *The Odyssey,* by Homer, are examples.
3. Virgil's *The Aeneid* is one; so is John Milton's *Paradise Lost.*

Epilogue
1. It is a piece of writing at the end of a literary work.
2. In a play, this may be used to summarize or comment on the main action.
3. Its antonym is *prologue.*

Exposition
1. This is usually short and comes at the beginning of the plot.
2. It is the part of the plot that provides necessary background information.
3. This beginning section can serve to introduce characters, the setting and the conflict.

Fantasy
1. This genre uses magic and other supernatural forms in the setting, characters, and/or the plot.
2. This genre includes events that could not happen in real life and often includes mythical beings.
3. Although similar to science fiction in some ways, this genre uses the supernatural rather than science or technology to explain events.

Figurative Language
1. In this type of language the words and phrases go beyond their literal meanings.
2. Prose, metaphor and personification are three common types of this kind of language.
3. Idioms are a form of this type of language.

Story Elements Bingo

Flashback 1. This narrative technique interrupts the chronological sequence of events to describe past events. 2. This technique can help the reader understand what is going on in the present by explaining what happened in the past. 3. This telling about past events can give the reader clues about a character's motivation.	**Foil** 1. It is a character who contrasts with another character, usually the protagonist. 2. The practical Sancho Panza is one; he is contrasted with the idealistic Don Quixote. 3. Dr. Watson is one; he is contrasted with Sherlock Holmes.
Foreshadowing 1. This refers to when an author drops hints about things that will occur later in the story. 2. Shakespeare used this technique in *Julius Caesar* when the soothsayer warns Caesar to beware the Ides of March. 3. Shakespeare used this technique in *Romeo and Juliet* when the characters say that they would rather die than live apart.	**Genres (Literary)** 1. It is a category of literature. 2. The three basic literary ones are poetry, drama, and prose. 3. Science fiction, historical fiction and mystery are three.
Historical Fiction 1. Works in this sub-genre of fiction try to capture the spirit, manners, and social conditions of the period in the past when the story takes place. 2. *Across Five Aprils* is an example of this sub-genre of fiction. 3. *My Brother Sam Is Dead* is an example of this sub-genre of fiction.	**Imagery** 1. This refers to the use of descriptive language that appeal to the readers' senses. 2. It is language that stimulates one or more of the senses: hearing, taste, touch, smell, or sight. 3. The following phrases in *The Call of the Wild,* by Jack London, exemplify this: **big** house; **sun-kissed**…Valley; **wide, cool** veranda; **green** pastures; and kept **cool** in the **hot** afternoon.
Inference 1. This refers to the act of coming to a conclusion based upon story clues and prior knowledge. 2. If you "read between the lines," you are making one. 3. If a character loses his beloved dog and you guess that he is sad, you are making one.	**Irony** 1. It refers to how something is not as it seems. There are several types, including verbal, dramatic and situational. 2. Verbal ___ is the use of words to express something other than and usually the opposite of the literal meaning. Sarcasm is an example. 3. Situational ___ is an outcome contrary to what was or might have been expected.
Literature 1. Fiction is ___ based upon the imagination. 2. Nonfiction is ___ based upon fact. 3. It comprises writings in prose or verse, especially those of high quality.	**Metaphor** 1. This is a comparison between two unlike things without the use of *like* or *as.* 2. This figure of speech says something *is* something else when in reality it is not. 3. An example of this figure of speech is found in *Little Women,* by Louisa May Alcott, when Jo calls Amy "a little goose."

Mood	**Narrator**
1. This literary element is the feeling the author creates for the readers. 2. It is the atmosphere or emotional condition created by the work. 3. This literary element is the general feeling the reader gets from reading the work.	1. In a work of fiction the story is told from his or her point of view. 2. It is someone who tells a story. 3. In *To Kill a Mockingbird,* Scout is this. The story is told from her point of view.
Novel	**Plot**
1. It is a complex fictional work in prose. 2. This work of prose is long enough to be divided into chapters. 3. Although the short story and this form of prose share many elements, the short story is not long enough to be divided into chapters.	1. It is the sequence of causal events in a story. 2. It can be divided into 5 parts: exposition, rising action, climax, falling action and dénouement. 3. It is a planned sequence of events with a beginning, a middle, and an end.
Point of View	**Prologue**
1. It is the perspective from which a story is told. 2. If a story is told from a first-person ___, one of the characters is telling the story. 3. If a story is told from a third-person ___, none of the characters is telling the story.	1. It is an introductory chapter to a literary work. 2. Its antonym is *epilogue.* 3. It comes from the Greek word *prologos,* which was the part of the play coming before the entrance of the chorus.
Prose	**Protagonist**
1. It is the language we use in everyday speech and writing. 2. Unlike poetry, it lacks the formal structure of meter or rhyme. 3. An epic is a form of poetry, but a novel is a form of ___.	1. It is the main character in a literary work. 2. Its antonym is *antagonist.* 3. It is the central character with whom the reader empathizes.
Satire	**Science Fiction**
1. It is a literary work that pokes fun at individual or societal weaknesses. 2. Although this literary genre is usually meant to be funny, its main purpose is to attack something of which the author disapproves. 3. In this genre the author uses wit and humor to poke fun at something and show disapproval.	1. This genre differs from fantasy because within the context of the story its imaginary elements are explained by science or technology. 2. Isaac Asimov and Robert A. Heinlein were well known authors in this genre. 3. If a literary work involves time travel, it is likely this genre.

Sequence 1. This refers to the ordering of events of a plot. 2. Chronological is the most common form of this. 3. Flashback is a break in the normal ___ of events in a story; it tells about events that occurred in the past.	**Setting** 1. It is the time, place and circumstance in which the story takes place. 2. The ___ of *Out of the Dust,* by Karen Hesse, is Oklahoma during the Dust Bowl of 1934. 3. The ___ of *Julie of the Wolves,* by Jean Craighead George, is the tundra of northern Alaska.
Stereotype 1. This kind of character has traits associated with a particular class or group of people. 2. This type of character is sometimes called a stock character. 3. The wicked stepmother is an example of this type of flat character.	**Style** 1. It refers to an author's manner of writing, including grammar, vocabulary, the use of figurative language and other factors. 2. Some elements of literary ___ include sentence structure, use of dialogue, vocabulary, point of view, character development, and tone. 3. Some general ones are straightforward, descriptive, scientific, and fanciful.
Subplot 1. This term refers to the secondary action of a story 2. This secondary action reinforces or contrasts with the main plot. 3. Sometimes two opening ones merge into a main plot.	**Suspense** 1. It is the quality that makes readers wonder what will happen next. 2. It is apprehension about what will happen. 3. Mysteries usually have this quality.
Symbol 1. It is the an object, character or idea used to represent something else. 2. Coffee is used as one to represent Jethro's coming of age in *Across Five Aprils,* by Irene Hunt,. 3. The mockingbird, used to represent innocence in *To Kill a Mockingbird,* by Harper Lee, is one.	**Theme** 1. It is the main idea of a literary work—the idea the author wants to convey. 2. The importance of family is a common one. 3. Good versus evil is a common one.
Tone 1. This literary element is the author's attitude toward the writing. 2. It may be serious, humorous, sarcastic, ironic, satirical, tongue-in-cheek, solemn, or objective. 3. Many confuse this with mood, but this is the writer's attitude toward what he or she is writing and mood is the feeling the reader gets when reading it.	**Traits** 1. When describing a character, we often refer to character ___. 2. If we say a character is loyal, kind, intelligent and honest, we are describing the character's positive character ___. 3. If we say a character is cruel, dishonest, and unreliable, we are describing the character's negative character ___.

Story Elements Bingo

Story Elements Bingo

Prose	Antagonist	Biography	Exposition	Characterization
Drama	Author	Suspense	Narrator	Setting
Theme	Science Fiction		Point of View	Tone
Subplot	Sequence	Style	Mood	Novel
Plot	Fantasy	Epic	Symbol	Metaphor

Story Elements Bingo

Subplot	Theme	Foil	Protagonist	Genres
Novel	Dialogue	Cliffhanger	Sequence	Literature
Connotation	Fantasy		Flashback	Style
Prologue	Satire	Science Fiction	Traits	Characterization
Setting	Suspense	Epic	Drama	Symbol

Story Elements Bingo

Fantasy	Style	Dialogue	Mood	Theme
Novel	Author	Climax	Antagonist	Irony
Sequence	Suspense		Literature	Allusion
Science Fiction	Connotation	Plot	Prologue	Foil
Symbol	Conflict	Epic	Traits	Genres

Story Elements Bingo: Card No. 3

© Barbara M Peller

Story Elements Bingo

Science Fiction	Literature	Biography	Conflict	Genres
Historical Fiction	Classics	Antagonist	Protagonist	Theme
Point of View	Prologue		Metaphor	Exposition
Style	Figurative Language	Suspense	Epic	Cliffhanger
Dénouement	Setting	Character	Symbol	Tone

Story Elements Bingo

Setting	Characterization	Sequence	Cliffhanger	Conflict
Historical Fiction	Style	Climax	Flashback	Author
Biography	Tone		Narrator	Imagery
Metaphor	Genres	Prose	Traits	Dialect
Dialogue	Epic	Theme	Science Fiction	Point of View

Story Elements Bingo: Card No. 5

Story Elements Bingo

Allusion	Literature	Foil	Genres	Tone
Mood	Sequence	Dialect	Antagonist	Theme
Protagonist	Dénouement		Classics	Flashback
Epic	Plot	Traits	Character	Biography
Novel	Cliffhanger	Prose	Point of View	Figurative Language

Story Elements Bingo

Prose	Literature	Imagery	Style	Dialogue
Novel	Genres	Fantasy	Author	Historical Fiction
Foil	Exposition		Flashback	Classics
Science Fiction	Prologue	Climax	Subplot	Connotation
Epic	Conflict	Traits	Character	Allusion

Story Elements Bingo

Point of View	Literature	Epilogue	Mood	Classics
Historical Fiction	Biography	Protagonist	Tone	Cliffhanger
Figurative Language	Conflict		Genres	Characterization
Symbol	Science Fiction	Subplot	Dénouement	Prologue
Suspense	Epic	Character	Sequence	Novel

Story Elements Bingo

Flashback	Dialogue	Fantasy	Figurative Language	Conflict
Dénouement	Genres	Point of View	Sequence	Literature
Irony	Prose		Author	Epilogue
Dialect	Characterization	Plot	Narrator	Imagery
Prologue	Traits	Climax	Subplot	Metaphor

Story Elements Bingo: Card No. 9

Story Elements Bingo

Subplot	Mood	Classics	Protagonist	Figurative Language
Tone	Cliffhanger	Antagonist	Author	Genres
Conflict	Literature		Exposition	Connotation
Plot	Metaphor	Dialect	Traits	Irony
Climax	Novel	Foil	Setting	Point of View

Story Elements Bingo

Allusion	Literature	Sequence	Dialect	Novel
Epilogue	Irony	Narrator	Flashback	Antagonist
Historical Fiction	Genres		Foil	Fantasy
Climax	Theme	Traits	Conflict	Subplot
Dénouement	Epic	Prose	Character	Dialogue

Story Elements Bingo: Card No. 11

© **Barbara M Peller**

Story Elements Bingo

Dialogue	Characterization	Irony	Mood	Flashback
Fantasy	Novel	Biography	Character	Author
Prose	Imagery		Tone	Protagonist
Epic	Prologue	Genres	Subplot	Historical Fiction
Literature	Epilogue	Conflict	Dénouement	Cliffhanger

Story Elements Bingo

Dialect	Characterization	Allusion	Irony	Tone
Biography	Epilogue	Genres	Flashback	Connotation
Mood	Cliffhanger		Fantasy	Imagery
Point of View	Traits	Classics	Conflict	Subplot
Epic	Metaphor	Character	Prose	Narrator

Story Elements Bingo: Card No. 13

Story Elements Bingo

Drama	Genres	Sequence	Flashback	Dénouement
Cliffhanger	Prose	Irony	Author	Literature
Dialect	Exposition		Foil	Climax
Metaphor	Traits	Conflict	Classics	Allusion
Epic	Protagonist	Connotation	Novel	Point of View

Story Elements Bingo

Narrator	Flashback	Sequence	Dialogue	Mood
Allusion	Foil	Antagonist	Biography	Dénouement
Tone	Prose		Theme	Literature
Epic	Irony	Epilogue	Traits	Dialect
Novel	Prologue	Character	Figurative Language	Fantasy

Story Elements Bingo: Card No. 15

Story Elements Bingo

Classics	Irony	Epilogue	Figurative Language	Satire
Protagonist	Connotation	Imagery	Historical Fiction	Exposition
Dialect	Characterization		Tone	Fantasy
Science Fiction	Cliffhanger	Epic	Narrator	Subplot
Dénouement	Stereotype	Character	Prologue	Literature

Story Elements Bingo

Climax	Inference	Foreshadowing	Irony	Drama
Narrator	Dénouement	Traits	Exposition	Imagery
Flashback	Point of View		Stereotype	Epilogue
Metaphor	Novel	Subplot	Sequence	Connotation
Plot	Dialect	Dialogue	Mood	Characterization

© **Barbara M Peller**

Story Elements Bingo

Figurative Language	Conflict	Cliffhanger	Dialect	Protagonist
Literature	Climax	Plot	Tone	Dénouement
Flashback	Connotation		Foreshadowing	Biography
Characterization	Antagonist	Traits	Subplot	Foil
Stereotype	Irony	Sequence	Inference	Allusion

© Barbara M Peller

Story Elements Bingo

Tone	Allusion	Irony	Epilogue	Subplot
Narrator	Mood	Literature	Dialogue	Exposition
Inference	Conflict		Author	Theme
Foil	Stereotype	Plot	Prologue	Foreshadowing
Biography	Satire	Novel	Point of View	Character

Story Elements Bingo

Drama	Inference	Mood	Irony	Character
Cliffhanger	Fantasy	Historical Fiction	Plot	Protagonist
Characterization	Imagery		Science Fiction	Antagonist
Setting	Suspense	Symbol	Prologue	Stereotype
Style	Point of View	Satire	Subplot	Foreshadowing

Story Elements Bingo

Narrator	Allusion	Historical Fiction	Irony	Setting
Characterization	Foreshadowing	Classics	Epilogue	Prose
Connotation	Novel		Inference	Sequence
Plot	Dialogue	Stereotype	Metaphor	Point of View
Science Fiction	Satire	Character	Climax	Prologue

Story Elements Bingo

Figurative Language	Foil	Foreshadowing	Biography	Dialect
Protagonist	Mood	Theme	Epilogue	Author
Cliffhanger	Exposition		Prose	Imagery
Stereotype	Metaphor	Prologue	Antagonist	Historical Fiction
Satire	Climax	Inference	Connotation	Foil

© **Barbara M Peller**

Story Elements Bingo

Classics	Inference	Dialogue	Biography	Character
Allusion	Drama	Novel	Narrator	Antagonist
Foil	Dialect		Symbol	Prose
Connotation	Satire	Stereotype	Climax	Prologue
Setting	Suspense	Point of View	Plot	Foreshadowing

Story Elements Bingo

Classics	Point of View	Drama	Inference	Epilogue
Foreshadowing	Character	Historical Fiction	Protagonist	Prose
Imagery	Figurative Language		Dialect	Connotation
Setting	Symbol	Stereotype	Climax	Characterization
Style	Science Fiction	Satire	Mood	Suspense

Story Elements Bingo

Science Fiction	Historical Fiction	Inference	Sequence	Foreshadowing
Antagonist	Characterization	Narrator	Classics	Author
Metaphor	Epilogue		Symbol	Stereotype
Theme	Setting	Suspense	Satire	Exposition
Character	Drama	Cliffhanger	Dénouement	Style

Story Elements Bingo: Card No. 25

Story Elements Bingo

Foreshadowing	Inference	Foil	Protagonist	Figurative Language
Plot	Mood	Epilogue	Drama	Classics
Metaphor	Symbol		Exposition	Science Fiction
Climax	Biography	Setting	Satire	Stereotype
Imagery	Dénouement	Sequence	Suspense	Style

Story Elements Bingo: Card No. 26

Story Elements Bingo

Foil	Cliffhanger	Inference	Drama	Fantasy
Setting	Symbol	Narrator	Stereotype	Author
Traits	Suspense		Satire	Science Fiction
Figurative Language	Allusion	Historical Fiction	Style	Antagonist
Dénouement	Exposition	Foreshadowing	Theme	Imagery

Story Elements Bingo

Foil	Drama	Theme	Inference	Classics
Fantasy	Foreshadowing	Symbol	Protagonist	Exposition
Suspense	Connotation		Imagery	Plot
Subplot	Figurative Language	Novel	Satire	Stereotype
Biography	Flashback	Dénouement	Style	Setting

Story Elements Bingo

Foreshadowing	Drama	Figurative Language	Narrator	Flashback
Prologue	Plot	Historical Fiction	Imagery	Theme
Metaphor	Symbol		Author	Inference
Fantasy	Setting	Genres	Satire	Stereotype
Classics	Epilogue	Style	Allusion	Suspense

Story Elements Bingo: Card No. 29

Story Elements Bingo

Conflict	Inference	Protagonist	Flashback	Stereotype
Antagonist	Drama	Foil	Exposition	Author
Metaphor	Dialect		Imagery	Historical Fiction
Style	Allusion	Biography	Satire	Symbol
Setting	Tone	Suspense	Foreshadowing	Theme